TYNDALE
H O U S E
PUBLISHERS
INCORPORATED

WHEATON
I L L I N O I S

Calligraphic word pictures inspired by the music and text of
GEORGE FREDERICK HANDEL'S

MESSIAH

with notes
by the artist

Timothy R Botts

ESPECIALLY FOR

Andrew Timothy, Jeremy Glen, & Catherine Elissa

Library of Congress Cataloging-in-Publication Data

Botts, Timothy R.,   date

    Calligraphic word pictures inspired by the music and text of
George Frederick Handel's Messiah / with notes by the artist,
Timothy R. Botts.

    p.   cm.

    Includes index.

    ISBN 0-8423-4235-4

    1. Calligraphy. 2. Handel, George Frederick, 1865-1759. Messiah.
I. Handel, George Frederick, 1865-1759. Messiah. 1991, II. Title.
III. Title: Messiah.

Z43.B727 1991

745.6'1977—dc20   *91-19660*

Printed in the United States of America

97 96 95 94 93 92 91

7   6   5   4   3   2

INTRODUCTION

I hope [Handel] will lay out his whole genius and skill upon it, that the composition may excel all his former compositions, as the subject excels every other subject. The subject is Messiah.

CHARLES JENNENS

With these words, George Frederick Handel's friend and supplier of lyrics predicted the greatness of the oratorio *Messiah*. The entire work was written between August 22 and September 14, 1741, and was first performed in Dublin on April 13, 1742, as a charity benefit. The sacred text of the Bible had inspired a genius to his highest capability.

Now, more than 250 years later, these Old and New Testament Scriptures, coupled with Handel's picturesque music, have inspired me to visually orchestrate *Messiah* through the medium of calligraphy. This is not a literal translation, for I am dwarfed by the composer's genius. But I hope the visual art will add a new dimension for you by capturing on the page your memory of the music and some of the power of the biblical text.

Jennens's introduction to the lyrics of *Messiah*, which is shown to the right, summarizes its theme.

*Majora Canamus
(Let us sing of greater things)*
VIRGIL

*And without controversy,
great is the mystery of godliness:
God was manifested in the flesh,
justified by the Spirit,
seen of angels,
preached among the Gentiles,
believed on in the world,
received up in glory.*
1 TIMOTHY 3:16

*In whom are hid all the treasures
of wisdom and knowledge.*
COLOSSIANS 2:3

PART ONE

Because of my interest in making words look like their meanings, I naturally related to Handel's picturesque music. In this opening recitative we learn that the Messiah's coming is for the sake of those who suffer. My job seemed to be to convey as much empathy in my art as the text and music express. The decision to use the horizontal format worked especially well here with the exceptionally long, drawn-out notes of the tenor.

comfort ye my people

SAITH YOUR GOD

speak ye comfortably to Jerusalem
AND CRY
UNTO HER
that her warfare is accomplished
that her iniquity is pardoned

The majority of *Messiah* is taken from the prophetic parts of the Bible. The announcement comes in marked contrast to the hopeless, oppressed condition of Israel—as surprising as an expressway appearing in the middle of the desert. Allowing the last word to run off the side of the page is my way of celebrating that the Lord has indeed come.

Pages 10-11: The melodic line expresses tremendous contrast in height and depth. The text speaks metaphorically of a major shake-up in the way the earth is structured. It brings to mind Jesus' teaching about the humble people who are given the kingdom of heaven. The pulsating first line of letters illustrates how I seek to wed artistic spontaneity in a subtle background with more dominant legible words on top.

Pages 12-13: As much as 80 percent of what we experience we experience through our eyes. Making a picture of this incredible announcement really increased the impact of the words for me. But I've learned when working with metaphors such as "mouth of the Lord" not to illustrate them too literally. Some visualization aids the imagination; too much stifles it.

A

FOR

The voice
of him,
that crieth
in the
Wilderness

PREPARE YE

THE WAY OF THE LORD

MAKE STRAIGHT

IN THE DESERT

HIGH WAY

OUR GOD

Every Valley
AND EVERY
AND HILL

shallbeexalted

the crooked straight
and the rough places plain
MOUNTAIN
MADE
LOW

GLORY OF THE LORD

THE GLORY OF THE LORD

THE GLORY OF THE LORD

THE GLORY OF THE LORD

THE GLORY OF THE LORD

THE GLORY OF THE LORD

AND ALL FLESH SHALL

AND ALL FLESH SHALL

AND ALL FLESH SHALL

AND ALL FLESH SHALL

AND ALL FLESH SHALL

ALL FLESH SHALL

ALL FLESH SHA

RD SHALL BE REVEALED
RD SHALL BE REVEALED
D SHALL BE REVEALED
SHALL BE REVEALED

for the mouth of the Lord hath spoken it

SEE IT TOGETHER
SEE IT TOGETHER
SEE IT TOGETHER
SEE IT TOGETHER
SEE IT TOGETHER

Thus saith the Lord of Hosts:
Yet once a little while and I will

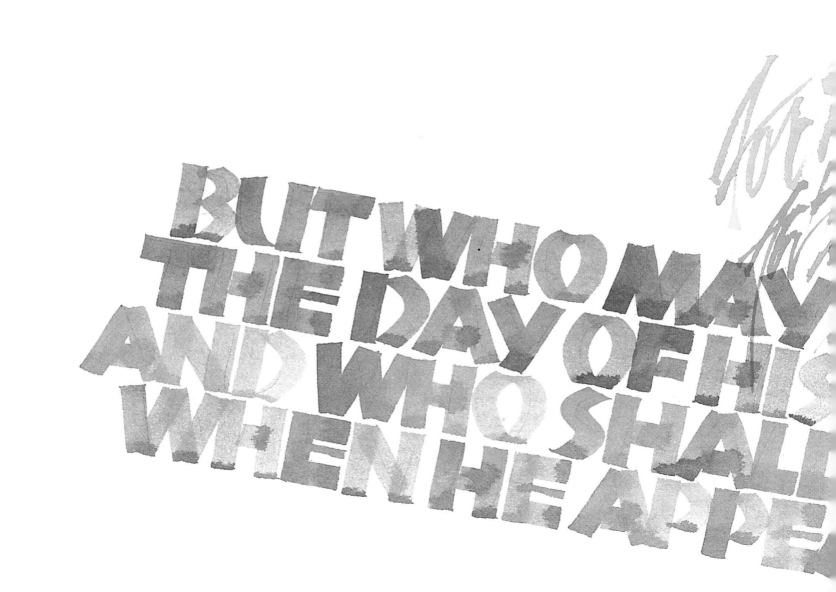

BUT WHO MAY
THE DAY OF HIS
AND WHO SHALL
WHEN HE APPE

Pages 14-15: By man's standards, there has often been a long time between God's announcements and their fulfillment. Here I contrast the time of waiting with the Lord's dramatic action. Three times the prophet declares, "He *shall* come."

Pages 16-17: There is a danger for Christian people who spend all their time in the New Testament. We miss the tremendous sense of awe for the holy character of God conveyed by the prophets. Here Handel's music runs as rampant as a forest fire, and I could not paint nearly as fast. But the multiple layering of words is a visual translation of the repeating choral lines, as well as the four singing parts.

This spread: In the design process I often look for natural patterns or coincidences. In this case I related the key word *righteousness* with the twelve-stone breastplate worn by the high priest (always a Levite) in Jewish history. God's character as the enabler is demonstrated in this verse—also His requirement that ministers be pure.

THAT THEY MAY

RIGHTEOUSNESS

OFFERING IN

OFFER UNTO

AN OFFERING

THE LORD

And He shall purify the sons of Levi

A beautiful metaphor throughout history for the birth of the Messiah has been a rose blooming. I chose this image because it also conveys the intimacy and fragility of God's choice to become one of us.

Pages 22-23: The direction of the lines of words was an instinctive choice for this loud and bold pronouncement. Afterward I saw a megaphone-like shape in the design. I remembered how sports fans also lift up their voices with strength. If we consider that the Jewish people were previously not permitted to see God, this prediction of Christ is certainly worth shouting about.

Pages 24-25: This text reminds me that the Jews were chosen first by God and that through the Messiah Gentiles gained acceptance. Knowledge of the truth is symbolized by light. But light is appreciated most in the face of darkness, in this case gross or unqualified darkness. So I use dark colors in my work, not to celebrate the dark side of life, but as a contrast with the light.

Behold, a virgin shall conceive, and bear a son, and shall call his name Emmanuel, God with us.

ARISE SHINE FOR THY LIGHT IS COME AND

O thou that tellest good tidings to Zion

get thee up into the high mountain

O thou that tellest good tidings to Jerusalem

lift up thy voice with strength

lift it up, be not afraid

Say unto the cities of Judah

BEHOLD YOUR

THE GLORY OF THE LORD IS RISEN UPON THEE

GOD

For darkness cover and gross the

but the lord shall arise upon thee

behold
shall
the earth
darkness
people

The people that walked in darkness and they that dwell in the shadow of death

have seen a great light
upon them hath the light shined

For unto us
a child is born
unto us a son is given
and the government
shall be upon His shoulder
and His name
shall be called

Wonder
COUNSELOR
The Mighty

THE EVERLAS

The prince

ful
God
TING FATHER
of peace

Pages 26-27: In response to the dramatic contrast of darkness and light in this text, Handel developed a unique movement back and forth between minor and major chords. The musical phrases also move from a wandering form to strong direction. I translated this into a metamorphosis of letter style, color, and direction.

Pages 28-29: This favorite foretelling of the first Christmas starts high on the page with God's giving and ends at the bottom with His peace to earth. When trying to illustrate words, I find it helpful to put them into my own words: *Wonderful* (He is much-loved), *Counselor* (He can help us), *The Mighty God* (God Himself), *The Everlasting Father* (He always exists), *Prince of Peace* (There is no peace without Him).

Pages 30-33: The challenge for me here was to show the contrast between the earthy shepherds and heaven's angels. Though a night scene is described, we are also told of a great light; so I opted for a white background. Notice that God chose to make His grand announcement to loyal, blue-collar workers on the night shift.

Once I determined to use a white background, I wrestled with how to show light on white. Through the intersection of many fine lines, I was able to capture a sparkling sensation. Handel's music is less than three minutes' duration in this section and dramatically describes the suddenness of the angelic appearance. I decided, however, that in my visual medium four pages were necessary to express the magnitude of the scene.

There were

AND LO! THE ANGEL OF THE LORD CAME UPON THEM

AND THE GLORY OF THE LORD SHONE ROUND ABOUT THEM

AND THEY WERE SORE AFRAID

AND THE ANGEL SAID UNTO THEM, FEAR NOT;

FOR BEHOLD, I BRING YOU GOOD TIDINGS OF GREAT JOY,

WHICH SHALL BE TO ALL PEOPLE,

FOR UNTO YOU IS BORN THIS DAY

IN THE CITY OF DAVID A SAVIOR

WHICH IS CHRIST THE LORD.

shepherds
abiding in the field,
keeping watch over their flocks
by night,

AND SUDDENLY
THERE WAS WITH THE ANGEL
A MULTITUDE OF THE HEAVENLY HOST
PRAISING GOD AND SAYING
GLORY
IN THE
AND PEACE
GOOD WILL

Handel borrowed a wedding gigue of his day as the basis for this text from the prophet Zechariah. How appropriate because Christ is described as the bridegroom of the Church in the New Testament. Such a joyful piece demanded a full range of colors. To maintain legibility, I reserved the lightest colors for less important parts of speech and for vowels and silent letters within significant words.

HE IS THE

RIGHTEOUS

SAVIOR

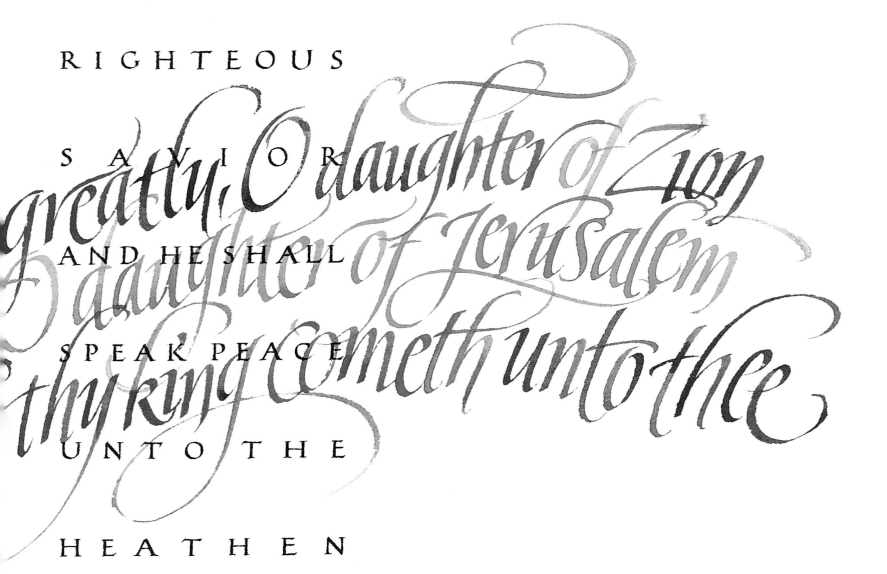

AND HE SHALL

SPEAK PEACE

UNTO THE

HEATHEN

greatly, O daughter of Zion, O daughter of Jerusalem thy king cometh unto thee

THEN SHALL THE EYES OF THE BLIND BE OPENED

The grammatical structure of a text is often the first clue to arranging it calligraphically. In this case there are four parallel descriptions of the healing work of the Messiah. By expressing these through visual metamorphoses, I was able to enter into the wonder of such miracles.

and then and the
the shall the tongue
ears lame of the
of the man dumb
deaf leap as shall
unstopped a hart sing

How often the Scriptures teach principles upside down from worldly standards! Here we find the Messiah likened to a shepherd who finds it worthwhile to identify with those who are vulnerable in society. I wanted to picture His ability to be in the midst of them and at the same time surrounding them.

Pages 40-41: I remember as a boy listening to this song and thinking it would never end. I guess I needed to experience the stress of adulthood to appreciate this wonderfully gentle, soothing melody. I also found that the slow tempo brought out of me some very relaxed letterforms.

He shall feed
His flock
like a

shepherd

and He shall gather the lambs with His arm
and carry them in His bosom
and gently lead those that are
with young

Come unto Him
all ye that labor
and are heavy laden
and He shall give you
Take His yoke upon you
and learn of Him
for He is meek and lowly of heart
and ye shall find rest to you

rest

our souls

The concept that was important for me to capture on paper was the reality of the Messiah's role in our lives. He did not come to end our trouble but to carry us through it. I wrestled with the paradox in this verse of light burdens. Drawing from my experience of air travel, my letterforms imitate the exhilarating weightlessness of clouds.

PART TWO

Pages 44-45: What fitting words to open the second part of the oratorio, which deals with the death of Christ. As I consider these prophecies and their fulfillment in the Gospels, I realize that this must be the most significant event in history. Handel's music eloquently expresses a monumental gravity that translated, for me, into a starkly simple composition. I wanted to show the awesome contrast between holy God and sinful man against the backdrop of the cross.

Pages 46-47: The music becomes painfully slow here with unaccompanied parts illustrating the utter desolation of the text. The Messiah's grief is set against the destructive noise of His accusers. Visually, then, I decided to lose the sorrowful words among the clamorous ones.

His yoke is easy

BURDEN

is light

BEHOLD THE

that taketh away

LAMB OF GOD

the sins of the world

Pages 48-49: God's justice and love meet in the foretelling of the Messiah's sacrifice for the sins of humanity. Handel seemed to feel the significance of the word *surely*. It describes the certainty of the prophecy fulfilled in Christ as well as the purposefulness of His passion.

This spread: The use of contrast is one of the artist's most powerful tools. The intensity of Christ's suffering is compared with its effective and all-encompassing results: our freedom and wholeness. By calligraphic standards, the flourishes are exaggerated, but they only begin to express the wonder of Christ's ability to work in our lives.

Pages 52-53: This book is not large enough to illustrate the awesome power of the closing lines of this piece. The music moves all over the staff and becomes increasingly complex. Perhaps this illustrates the entanglement that results from our wanderings.

we are healed

All we like sheep have gone e

All we like sheep

All we like sheep have

All we like sheep have astray

All we like sheep gone

All we like sheep p

All we like sheep astray

All we like sheep ha

All we like sheep have

we ke sheep ha have

sheep have

and the Lord ha

the iniqu

All we like sheep have gone astray; we have turned every one to his own way; and the LORD hath laid on Him the iniquity of us all.

The wandering sheep have now organized, and the sight is not pretty. The psalmist's description is so graphic—all that is needed is for my emotions to pay attention. The biting sarcasm of the chorus translates into sharply exaggerated serifs or endings to the letters.

Pages 56-57: One of the challenges for me in doing this book was not only to paint each musical piece but also to weave each of them together into a unity of the whole. In this case, the transition was the text's reference to the previous ridicule, which leads into the Messiah's deep sorrow. The words on the page sink to their lowest point.

Thy rebuke hath broken his heart

He looked for some to have pity on him, but there was no man, neither found he any to comfort him

BE

This technique of wetting the paper before writing requires working quite fast. If the paper is too wet, the letters blur beyond recognition. If one waits too long, the letters begin to form hard edges.

Behold is a word that simply commands us to take notice. One of the unique gifts of an artist—developed through time and patience—is to be able to see things that other people miss. But gifts are best shared, and it brings me great fulfillment when my art helps another person grab hold of a spiritual truth.

58

HOLD

and see if there be
any sorrow
like unto
His sorrow

Unlike most of the other spreads, these two pieces are positioned with a distinct separation between them. This marks the point of the Messiah's death. Yet the assurance of His resurrection immediately follows.

Pages 62-63: This strongly horizontal composition in multiple layers echoes the repetition in the lyrics as well as the buildup in the musical score. "Heads lifted up" reminded me of this less familiar calligraphic style with its unusually long ascenders from the time of Charlemagne in the eighth century. I tried to maintain some direction for the reader by the use of alternately colored lines. Nevertheless, by the end of the piece we are caught up in the emotion of glory for which words are inadequate.

Pages 64-65: This calligraphic style is based on Legend, a typeface reminiscent of Arabic writing. I exaggerated their backhand forms to roll the way clouds move across the sky. The use of multiple layers suggests the enormity of the heavenly host.

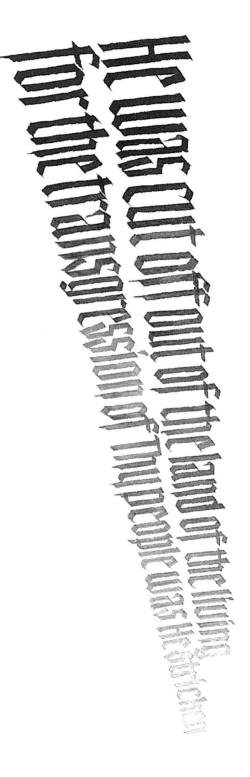

But Thou didst not leave His soul in hell, nor didst Thou suffer Thy Holy One to see corruption

Lift up your heads, O ye gates;

Lift up your heads, O ye gates;

and be ye lift up, ye everlasting

and be ye lift up

and the King of glory

and the

Who is the King

Who is the

The Lord strong

The Lord

The Lord mig

He is the Ki

oors;
e everlasting doors;
hall come in.
King of glory shall come in.
of glory?
King of glory?
nd mighty,
f Hosts,
hty in battle
ng of glory.

UNTO WHICH
OF THE ANGELS
SAID HE AT ANY TIME,
THOU ART MY SON,
THIS DAY HAVE
I BEGOTTEN THEE?

Let all the angels

on

high

captive

captivity

led

for

men

gifts

received

enemies

among

them

might

dwell

THE LORD GAVE THE WORD GREAT WAS THE COMPANY OF THE PREACHERS

THE COMPANY OF THE PREACHERS
THE COMPANY OF THE PREACHERS
THE COMPANY OF THE PREACHERS
THE COMPANY OF THE PREACHERS
THE COMPANY OF THE PREACHERS
WAS THE COMPANY OF THE PREACHE
THE COMPANY OF THE PREACHERS
THE COMPANY OF THE PREACHERS
WAS THE COMPANY OF THE PREACHERS
WAS THE COMPANY OF THE PREACHERS
WAS THE COMPANY OF THE PREACHERS
WAS THE COMPANY OF THE PREACHERS
THE COMPANY OF THE PREACHERS
THE COMPANY OF THE PREACHE
HE COMPANY OF THE PREACHE
OMPANY OF THE PREAC
COMPANY OF THE PREA
PANY OF TH
A

Pages 66-67: Handel's music becomes playful to celebrate Christ's ascension and new relationship with humanity. These bouquets of letters are my visual representation of His gifts distributed to us. Meanwhile, His invisible presence quietly encircles the background.

Pages 68-69: After making this word picture, I became aware of how important is the source of a message, especially as a unifying force. The faithfulness of preachers is important also if the light is to be fully transmitted. Twenty centuries of preaching the gospel in more than two hundred countries of the world is interpreted by the energy of Handel's music.

This spread: Some of the most beautiful people I know are missionaries of the gospel. There is a loneliness about this melody much like the path they are called to travel. Just as missionaries do not bring attention to themselves, I have placed the visual emphasis on their message.

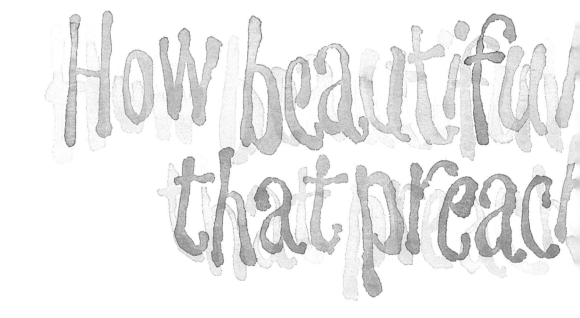

AND BRING GLAD TIDINGS

are the feet of them

OF

GOOD THINGS

the gospel of peace

THEIR SOUND

IS GONE OUT

INTO ALL LANDS

AND

THEIR WOR

S

UNTO

THE ENDS OF

THE WORLD

Pages 72-73: Up and down the scale the music runs like sound waves over the circumference of the earth. My love for letterforms comes through here with the bands of alphabets from around the world. They begin with the original languages of the Bible: Hebrew and Greek. Portions of the Bible are translated in over one thousand different languages to date.

This spread: Despite the glory of the Messiah in the former passages, we come to this account of the present age of unbelief and persecution. How keenly I felt the impact of this verse as I completed its final art during the war with Iraq.

Pages 76-77: Traditional calligraphic composition calls for the letters to be placed in the center of the page with generous white space around them. But this statement of rebellion called for breaking with convention. The image in my mind was of revolving words flung out of orbit.

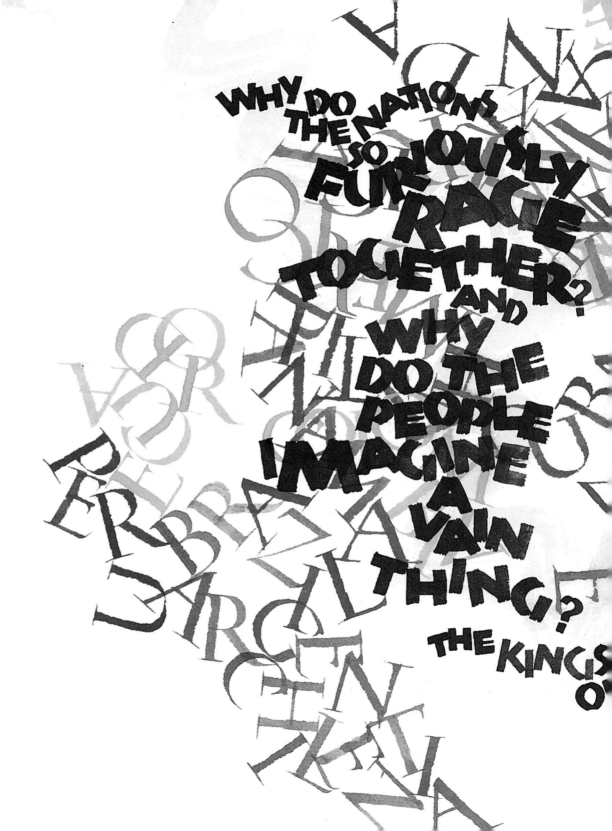

Let us
break
their bonds
asunder
and cast away
their yokes
from us

HE
THAT
DWELLETH
IN HEAVEN
SHALL
THE
LORD
SHALL

THOU SHALT
THOU SHALT BREAK
THOU SHALT DASH

LIKE A POT

With them to Scorn
in Derusion
THEM A ROD OF IRON
THEM WITH A ROD OF IRON
THEM IN PIECES
TERS VESSEL

Pages 78-79: With these two numbers we discover that the Lord has the last laugh! Handel might have been at a loss, as I was, to portray the Most High in vengeful laughter. He wrote just four bars of music. The challenge in the second verse was to maintain legibility while deliberately fragmenting the letters. We feel the utter foolishness of battling the Almighty.

Pages 81-87: The word *hallelujah* belongs to Jews and Christians and can be recognized in most languages. It is a call to praise Yahweh or Jehovah. Before the chorus ends, the word is heard more than fifty times. Just as calligraphers in the classic tradition have sought to balance spontaneity with structure, Handel gives us breathtaking jubilation without losing control.

Hallelujah

FOR THE LORD GOD OMNIPOTENT REIGNETH

FOR THE LORD GOD OMNIPOTENT

FOR THE LORD GOD OMNIPOTENT

FOR THE LORD GOD OMNIP OT

FOR THE LORD GOD OMNIPOTENT

Hal

FOR THE LORD GOD OMN

FOR THE LORD

FOR THE LORD GO

FOR THE LORD

REIGNETH

OMNIPOTENT

Hallelujah

Hallelujah

THE
KINGDOM
OF THIS
WORLD
IS BECOME
THE KING
OF OUR
AND OF
HIS CH

OM

ORD *and He* shall reign foreve

RIST

Halle

KING OF KINGS
LORD OF LOR

PART THREE

Job's remarkable testimony of hope parallels that of Christian believers today who at their greatest point of need receive God's grace. Notice how much more frank the Bible is than our current society in describing death. My favorite part of this design is the New Testament verse in green passing through the *h* in *earth*. It symbolizes Christ's passage from death into life.

Pages 90-91: Just as different as death and life are Handel's distinct halves of this music. No transition here, only stark contrast. I used space on the left the way Handel used a cappella. We feel the seeming hopelessness of death. Then he breaks into the major key, which was my cue to get out the colors.

I KNOW THAT
MY REDEEMER LIVETH
AND THAT
HE SHALL STAND
AT THE LATTER DAY.
UPON THE EARTH

For now is Christ risen from the dead

and though worms
destroy this body

the first fruits of them that sleep

YET
IN
MY FLESH
SHALL I SEE GOD

since by man came death

for as in Adam all die

by man came also the resurrection of the dead
even so in Christ shall all be made alive

At this point I moved to the experimental, breaking traditional calligraphic rules to try to create new forms. This parallels the mystery of the future described in the text. First the letters are squeezed as if to barely let light through. Next they stretch out as if yawning. Then they slope to a sudden climax of angled forms without any curves.

Pages 94-95: The strength of the future imperative is reinforced by Handel's vigorous music for trumpet and bass voice. What a challenge to try to picture what we have not yet seen or experienced!

Behold I tell you a mystery we shall not all sleep but we shall all be changed in a moment in the twinkling of an eye At THE LAST TRUMPET

THE TRUMPET SHALL SOUND
and the dead shall be raised i[n]
and we shall be CHA[N]
for this corruptible must put on [in]
and this mortal must put on im[mortality]

corruptible

incorruptible

mortality

The transition between this spread and
the following is an expression of the
power of Christ's resurrection. I
thought about the force of an airplane
taking off when I made the tail of the *y*
in *victory*. The use of sarcasm in the
verse on page 99 is not often found in
the biblical text. This seemed to call
for some nasty-looking letters.

THEN SHALL BE
BROUGHT TO PASS
THE SAYING THAT
IS WRITTEN:

is swallowed up in Victory

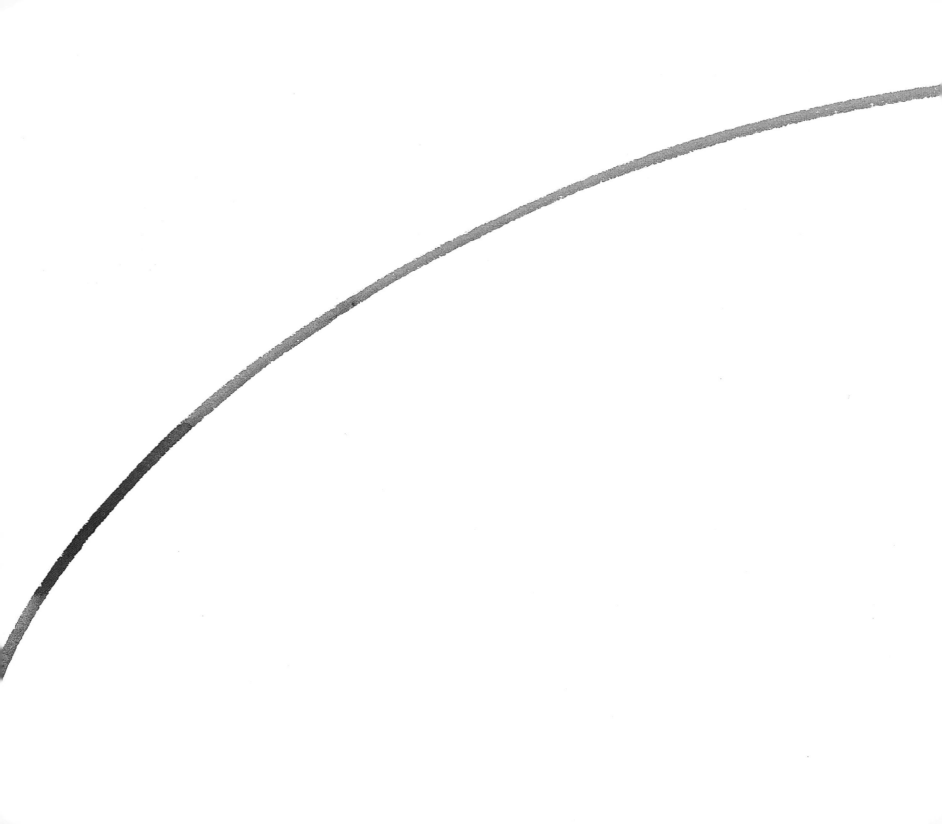

O DEATH
THY WHERE IS
THY STING?
O GRAVE
WHERE IS
THY VICTORY?
THE STING
OF DEATH IS SIN,
AND
THE STRENGTH
OF SIN
IS
THE LAW

The wonderful spontaneity of this melody reminds me of the ecstasy of receiving an extraordinary gift. I had this feeling when our children were born, when I held my first published book in my hands, and the time I saw a rainbow arc the entire sky. But appropriately we celebrate here the final contest of history.

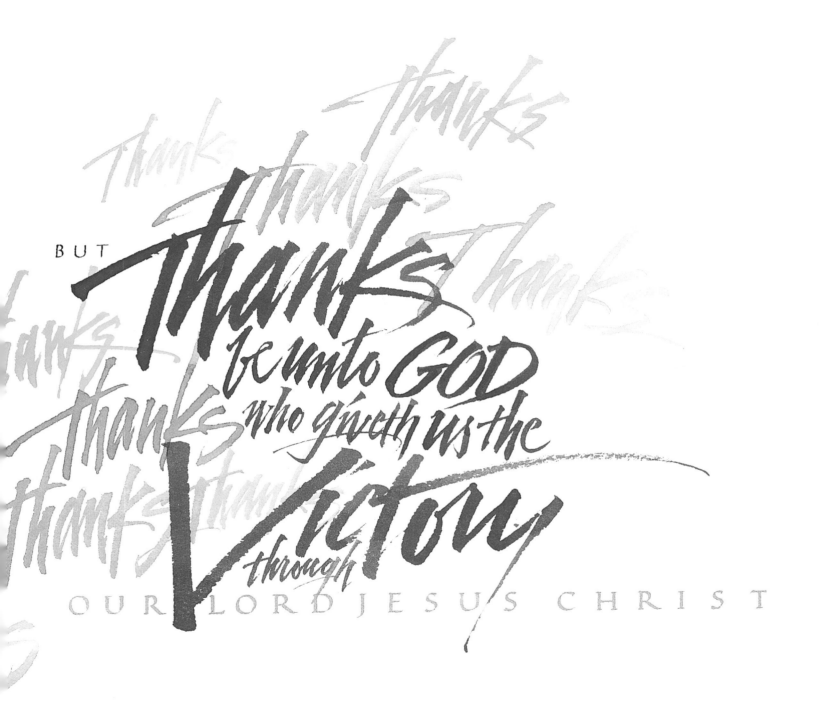

BUT Thanks be unto GOD who giveth us the Victory through

OUR LORD JESUS CHRIST

The Christian Church is built on the strength of God's commitment to those who belong to Him. Our self-image is forever settled in these verses. Drawing again on the principles of contrast, the delicate flourishes pervade the blocks of letters even as Christ mysteriously relates to each of us.

Pages 104-109: Calligraphic flourishes, and the great music of Handel, have their basis in glory. Robert Henri, the highly esteemed French teacher of painting, said: "Everything depends upon the attitude of the artist toward his subject." Oh for our culture to again recognize the glory of the Lord and His creation! The music and the words end here, but for those of us who believe, the real event in heaven will continue forever.

IF IT IS GOD WHO JUSTIFIETH, WHO IS HE THAT CONDEMNETH?

IT IS CHRIST THAT DIED, YEA, RATHER, THAT IS RISEN AGAIN, WHO IS AT THE RIGHT HAND OF GOD who makes intercession for us,

GOD BE FOR US WHO CAN BE AGAINST US?

WHO SHALL LAY ANY THING CHARGE OF GOD'S ELECT?

WORTHY
IS THE LAMB
THAT WAS SLAIN
AND HATH REDEEMED US
TO GOD BY HIS BLOOD

BLESSING
GLORY
HONOR
[ST]RENGTH
[KINGD]OM

AM·EN

INDEX